Freedom In Capitalism

Nations Wealth In The Hands Of The People Of A Democratic System In The Twenty-First Century

Greg V. Jack

Copyright © 2024

Greg V. Jack

All rights reserved. No part of this publication may be reproduced, distributed, or transmitted in any form or by any means, including photocopying, recording, or other electronic or mechanical methods, without the prior written permission of the publisher, except in the case of brief quotations embodied in critical reviews and certain other noncommercial uses permitted by copyright law.

- Introduction 4
  - Chapter 1 8
    - Historical Context 8
    - Economic Principles 15
  - **Chapter 2: The Case for Capitalism** 22
    - Economic Efficiency 22
    - Innovation and Entrepreneurship 27
    - Individual Freedom 31
  - **Chapter 3: Capitalism in Practice** 38
    - Market Mechanisms 38
    - Role of Government 45
    - Regulation and Deregulation 52
  - **Chapter 4: The Moral Dimension** 59
    - Capitalism and Ethics 61
    - Social Responsibility 68
    - Wealth Distribution 73
  - **Chapter 5: Challenges and Criticisms** 79
    - Inequality 79
    - Environmental Impact 86
    - Globalization 93
  - **Chapter 6: The Future of Capitalism** 100
    - Adapting to Change 102
    - Technological Advances 107
    - Global Perspectives 112
  - **Chapter 7: Capitalism and Society** 117
    - Education and Opportunity 119
    - Healthcare and Welfare 124
    - Culture and Media 130
- **Conclusion** 136

Introduction

In a world marked by diverse economic ideologies and political systems, the quest for freedom stands as a timeless aspiration of humanity. Rooted in the principles of autonomy, self-determination, and individual agency, freedom is a fundamental value that underpins our societies and shapes our collective destiny. Yet, amidst the complexities of modern capitalism, the question arises: does capitalism truly foster freedom, or does it impose constraints and inequalities that undermine its very essence?

In "Freedom in Capitalism," we embark on a profound exploration of this critical inquiry, delving into the intricate relationship between freedom and capitalism. Through a compelling blend of historical analysis and economic theory this book seeks to unravel the complexities of freedom within capitalist frameworks, shedding light on its multifaceted manifestations and implications for society.

At its core, capitalism represents a dynamic economic system characterized by private ownership, free markets, and the pursuit of profit. It offers individuals unparalleled opportunities for innovation, entrepreneurship, and economic autonomy, unleashing the creative potential of human ingenuity and fostering unprecedented levels of prosperity and progress. In capitalist societies, individuals are afforded the freedom to pursue their own economic interests, make autonomous choices, and chart their own paths to success.

However, the story of freedom in capitalism is far from straightforward. While capitalism promises freedom and opportunity for some, it also perpetuates inequalities and injustices that restrict the freedoms of others. The concentration of wealth and power in the hands of a privileged few can limit the economic opportunities and social mobility of marginalized groups, perpetuating cycles of poverty and exclusion. Moreover, the pursuit of profit in capitalist economies can sometimes come at the expense of human dignity, environmental sustainability, and social cohesion, raising profound ethical questions about the true meaning of freedom within capitalist frameworks.

Against this backdrop, "Freedom in Capitalism" seeks to navigate the complexities of freedom within capitalist societies, exploring how economic systems shape individual liberties and societal dynamics. By critically examining the historical, economic, and philosophical dimensions of freedom in capitalism, this book aims to deepen our understanding of its complexities and implications for society. Through rigorous analysis and thought-provoking insights, "Freedom in Capitalism" challenges us to confront the tensions and contradictions inherent in capitalist systems and reimagines the possibilities for freedom and justice.

Chapter 1: The Foundations of Capitalism

The foundations of capitalism delve deep into the historical and economic underpinnings that have shaped this socio-economic system. Understanding these foundations is crucial for comprehending the essence of capitalism and its implications for society. Here, we'll explore various aspects that contribute to the foundations of capitalism.

Historical Context

Capitalism, as an economic and social system, has a rich and complex historical context that spans centuries. Its roots can be traced back to the emergence of trade and commerce in ancient civilizations, but it evolved significantly over time, especially during the transition from feudalism to modern industrial society. To understand the historical context of capitalism, we must examine its key developments and influences throughout history. Here are some histories about capitalism.

Early Economic Systems: Before capitalism, various economic systems existed. In ancient societies such as Mesopotamia, Egypt, Greece, and Rome, economies were primarily agrarian, with trade occurring through barter systems and primitive markets. Wealth and power were often concentrated in the hands of monarchs, aristocrats, or religious institutions.

Medieval Feudalism: The feudal system dominated Europe during the Middle Ages. It was characterized by a hierarchical structure in which land was granted by monarchs to nobles in exchange for military service and loyalty. Peasants worked the land in exchange for protection and the right to use the land. Economic activity was largely localized, with limited trade and little economic mobility.

Commercial Revolution: The late Middle Ages and the Renaissance witnessed the beginnings of a commercial revolution in Europe. Increased trade with the East, facilitated by the Crusades and the Silk Road, led to the growth of merchant class and urban centers. The rise of banking, the spread of double-entry bookkeeping, and the establishment of joint-stock companies laid the groundwork for capitalist practices.

Age of Exploration and Mercantilism: The 15th and 16th centuries saw European powers embarking on voyages of exploration, seeking new trade routes and sources of wealth. Mercantilism emerged as the dominant economic policy, emphasizing state intervention in the economy to maximize exports and accumulate precious metals. Colonies were established to exploit resources and provide markets for manufactured goods.

Industrial Revolution: The Industrial Revolution, which began in Britain in the late 18th century, marked a transformative period in human history. It was characterized by the mechanization of production, the shift from agrarian to industrial economies, and the growth of urbanization. Innovations such as the steam engine, textile machinery, and iron smelting revolutionized production processes, leading to increased efficiency and productivity.

Capitalist Ideologies: The Industrial Revolution also saw the emergence of capitalist ideologies, notably classical liberalism and laissez-faire economics. Thinkers such as Adam Smith, David Ricardo, and John Stuart Mill argued for the virtues of free markets, competition, and limited government intervention. Smith's seminal work, "The Wealth of Nations" (1776), laid the intellectual foundation for capitalism as an economic system based on self-interest and the division of labor.

Rise of Capitalist Economies: Capitalism spread rapidly across Europe and North America during the 19th century, fueled by industrialization, technological innovation, and globalization. The development of railways, telegraphs, and steamships facilitated trade and communication on a global scale. Capitalists amassed wealth through ownership of factories, mines, and railroads, while laborers faced harsh working conditions and exploitation.

Twentieth Century Capitalism: The 20th century witnessed the expansion and evolution of capitalism, alongside periods of economic crisis and reform. The Great Depression of the 1930s prompted governments to adopt Keynesian economics, advocating for state intervention to stabilize economies through fiscal and monetary policies. The post-World War II era saw the rise of welfare states in Western Europe and the establishment of mixed economies blending market principles with social welfare programs.

Globalization and Neoliberalism: The late 20th century saw the resurgence of free-market capitalism with the rise of neoliberalism. Neoliberal policies advocated for deregulation, privatization, and free trade, aiming to unleash market forces and promote economic efficiency. Globalization intensified economic interconnectedness, with multinational corporations dominating global markets and production networks.

Contemporary Challenges: Despite its successes, capitalism faces numerous challenges in the 21st century. Rising inequality, environmental degradation, and financial instability have led to calls for reform and alternative economic models. Debates rage over the role of government regulation, social safety nets, and the balance between economic growth and sustainability.

The historical context of capitalism is a narrative of transformation and upheaval, shaped by technological progress, economic theories, and social movements. From its origins in ancient trade to its current manifestations in a globalized world, capitalism continues to evolve and adapt, leaving a profound impact on societies and economies worldwide. Understanding this historical context is essential for grappling with the complexities and contradictions of the capitalist system.

Economic Principles

Capitalism is an economic system in which the means of production and distribution of goods and services are privately owned for the purpose of creating utility and making profit. This determine the operation of economic activities and how goods and services are distributed. Here, I'll delve extensively into the key economic principles of capitalism:

1. Private Property Rights: Central to capitalism is the concept of private property rights. Individuals, businesses, and corporations have the right to own, use, and dispose of property and resources as they see fit. This includes land, capital goods, intellectual property, and other assets. Private property rights provide incentives for investment, innovation, and efficient resource allocation by allowing individuals to reap the benefits of their efforts.

2. Market Economy: Capitalism relies on market mechanisms to allocate resources and determine prices. In a market economy, goods and services are produced, bought, and sold based on supply and demand in competitive markets. Prices serve as signals that convey information about scarcity, preferences, and production costs, guiding producers and consumers in their decision-making. Market competition incentivizes efficiency, innovation, and responsiveness to consumer demands.

3. Profit Motive: The pursuit of profit is a driving force in capitalism. Entrepreneurs, businesses, and investors seek to maximize profits by producing goods and services that are in demand and selling them at prices higher than the cost of production. Profit acts as an incentive for risk-taking, innovation, and investment in productive activities. It signals market opportunities and directs resources toward their most valued uses.

4. Division of Labor and Specialization: Capitalism promotes the division of labor and specialization, whereby individuals and businesses focus on producing specific goods or services in which they have a comparative advantage. Specialization increases productivity by allowing workers to develop expertise and efficiency in their respective tasks. This leads to economies of scale, lower production costs, and higher overall output.

5. Free Enterprise: Capitalism embraces the principle of free enterprise, which entails minimal government interference in economic activities. Businesses are free to enter and exit markets, make independent decisions regarding production and pricing, and compete with one another based on quality, price, and innovation. Free enterprise fosters entrepreneurship, creativity, and flexibility, enabling markets to adapt to changing conditions and consumer preferences.

6. Voluntary Exchange: Transactions in capitalism are based on voluntary exchange, where individuals and businesses engage in trade for mutual benefit. Buyers and sellers freely negotiate terms of exchange, including prices, quantities, and conditions. Voluntary exchange ensures that transactions are consensual and that both parties perceive themselves as better off as a result. It promotes efficiency by allowing resources to flow to their most valued uses.

7. Consumer Sovereignty: In capitalist economies, consumer preferences drive production decisions through the principle of consumer sovereignty. Businesses respond to consumer demand by producing goods and services that satisfy consumer preferences and maximize utility. Consumer sovereignty ensures that resources are allocated efficiently to produce the goods and services that society values most, as determined by consumer choices in the marketplace.

8. Limited Government Intervention: While capitalism emphasizes free markets and individual freedom, it also recognizes the need for some government intervention to ensure the proper functioning of the economy. Government intervention may include enforcing property rights, regulating markets to prevent monopolies or unfair practices, providing public goods and services, and addressing market failures such as externalities and information asymmetry. However, the extent of government intervention varies depending on the economic ideology and policy preferences of a given society.

9. Price Mechanism: Prices play a crucial role in capitalism as signals that convey information about relative scarcity and value. Prices are determined through the interaction of supply and demand in competitive markets. They reflect the underlying costs of production, consumer preferences, changes in supply and

demand conditions, and other market factors. The price mechanism allocates resources efficiently by guiding producers and consumers in their decision-making, ensuring that resources are directed to their most productive uses.

10. Dynamic Nature: Capitalism is inherently dynamic and adaptive, characterized by constant innovation, technological change, and creative destruction. Entrepreneurs and businesses compete to introduce new products, processes, and technologies that improve efficiency, lower costs, and create value for consumers. Creative destruction refers to the process whereby obsolete industries and technologies are replaced by newer, more efficient ones, driving economic progress and growth over time.

In a nutshell, the economic principles of capitalism revolve around private property rights, market competition, the profit motive, specialization, free enterprise, voluntary exchange, consumer sovereignty, limited government intervention, the price mechanism, and dynamic innovation. These principles interact to shape the behavior of individuals and businesses, allocate resources efficiently, and drive economic growth and prosperity within capitalist societies.

Chapter 2: The Case for Capitalism

The case for capitalism rests on its ability to promote economic growth, innovation, individual freedom, and prosperity. Advocates argue that capitalism, with its emphasis on free markets, private property rights, and limited government intervention, offers the most efficient and equitable means of organizing economic activity. Here's a detailed exploration of the case for capitalism

Economic Efficiency

Economic efficiency is a cornerstone of the case for capitalism, as it represents the system's ability to allocate resources optimally, maximize production, and enhance overall welfare. At its core, capitalism is founded on the principles of free markets, competition, and the pursuit of profit, which collectively work to promote efficiency in resource allocation and economic decision-making.

In capitalist economies, resources are allocated through market mechanisms such as supply and demand, prices, and competition. These market forces provide valuable information about consumer preferences, resource scarcity, and production costs, guiding producers and consumers in their decision-making processes. Prices serve as signals that convey information, guiding resources to their most valued uses and ensuring that goods and services are allocated efficiently.

Competition is another key driver of economic efficiency in capitalism. Firms compete with one another to attract customers, improve product quality, and lower prices. This competitive pressure incentivizes firms to innovate, invest in research and development, and adopt more efficient production techniques. In competitive markets, inefficient firms are driven out of the market, while more efficient firms thrive, leading to greater overall efficiency in resource allocation.

The pursuit of profit is a fundamental incentive in capitalism that drives economic efficiency. Entrepreneurs and businesses seek to maximize profits by minimizing costs and maximizing revenues. The profit motive encourages firms to allocate resources efficiently, invest in productive activities, and innovate to gain a competitive edge. Profit signals market opportunities and guides resource allocation, ensuring that resources are directed towards their most valued uses.

Capitalism also promotes specialization and division of labor, which contribute to economic efficiency. Specialization allows individuals and firms to focus on producing goods and services in which they have a comparative advantage, leading to higher productivity and output. By specializing in specific tasks or industries, individuals and firms can achieve economies of scale, lower production costs, and increase overall efficiency.

Moreover, capitalism encourages flexibility and adaptability, allowing resources to be reallocated quickly in response to changing market conditions. Capital markets efficiently allocate capital to its most productive uses, channeling resources to entrepreneurs and businesses with promising ideas and growth potential.

Strong property rights and the rule of law are essential for promoting economic efficiency in capitalism. The rule of law ensures that contracts are enforced, disputes are resolved impartially, and individuals and businesses can operate in a stable and predictable legal environment, reducing transaction costs and fostering economic exchange.

Economic efficiency is a central tenet of the case for capitalism. Through market mechanisms, competition, the pursuit of profit, specialization, flexibility, and strong institutions, capitalism promotes efficiency in resource allocation and economic decision-making, leading to higher levels of productivity, economic growth, and overall welfare.

Innovation and Entrepreneurship

Innovation and entrepreneurship are not just incidental features of capitalism, they are intrinsic to its very essence. Creative destruction describes the process by which new innovations and entrepreneurial ventures disrupt existing industries and business models, leading to the replacement of obsolete technologies and practices with newer, more efficient ones.

Capitalism's foundation in free markets and competition creates fertile ground for innovation to thrive. In a capitalist system, entrepreneurs are free to pursue new ideas, start businesses, and compete with established firms. This freedom unleashes human creativity, ingenuity, and ambition, driving a constant cycle of innovation and improvement.

Entrepreneurs play a central role in this process. They are the trailblazers who identify market opportunities, take risks, and transform ideas into reality. Whether it's a small-scale startup or a multinational corporation, entrepreneurship drives economic growth by creating new products, services, and industries.

Innovation and entrepreneurship are not limited to technology and business processes; they also encompass social and organizational innovation. Capitalism encourages experimentation and adaptation, leading to the development of new organizational structures, management practices, and ways of doing business. These innovations contribute to productivity gains, efficiency improvements, and increased competitiveness in the marketplace.

Moreover, capitalism's emphasis on property rights and the rule of law provides a stable and supportive environment for innovation and entrepreneurship to flourish. Secure property rights protect intellectual property, giving innovators the confidence to invest in research and development without fear of expropriation or infringement. The rule of law ensures that contracts are enforced, disputes are resolved impartially, and entrepreneurs can operate in a predictable legal environment, reducing uncertainty and encouraging investment in innovation.

Innovation and entrepreneurship are not just drivers of economic growth; they are also catalysts for social progress and human development. They create jobs, expand opportunities, and empower individuals to pursue their dreams and aspirations. By promoting innovation and entrepreneurship, capitalism unleashes the potential of individuals and societies to achieve greater prosperity, resilience, and well-being.

Innovation and entrepreneurship are integral to the case for capitalism. They embody capitalism's dynamic, adaptive, and forward-thinking nature, driving economic growth, technological progress, and societal development. By fostering an environment where innovation and entrepreneurship can thrive, capitalism unleashes human potential and creates opportunities for individuals and societies to flourish.

Individual Freedom

Individual freedom stands as a fundamental pillar of the case for capitalism, embodying the principle that individuals possess the autonomy to make choices regarding their own lives, pursuits, and economic activities. In capitalist societies, individual freedom permeates various aspects of life, ranging from personal decisions to economic endeavors, underpinned by the belief that individuals are best equipped to determine their own paths and pursue their own interests.

At its core, capitalism champions the freedom of choice, allowing individuals to make decisions based on their preferences, desires, and values. This freedom extends to economic decisions, enabling individuals to choose their occupations, pursue entrepreneurial ventures, and engage in voluntary transactions with others. In a capitalist system, individuals are not bound by predetermined roles or centrally imposed directives; rather, they have the liberty to chart their own course and shape their own destinies.

Moreover, capitalism safeguards individual freedom through the protection of property rights and the rule of law. Secure property rights ensure that individuals have ownership and control over their possessions, including land, capital, and intellectual property. This protection empowers individuals to utilize their resources as they see fit, whether it be starting a business, investing in innovation, or saving for the future. The rule of law ensures that contracts are enforced, disputes are resolved impartially, and individuals are treated equally under the law, providing a stable and predictable legal framework for economic and personal activities.

In capitalist societies, economic freedom and individual liberty are intricately intertwined. Economic freedom allows individuals to engage in voluntary exchange, compete in markets, and pursue their economic interests without undue interference from government or external actors. This freedom empowers individuals to harness their entrepreneurial spirit, take risks, and innovate, driving economic growth and prosperity. Moreover, economic freedom fosters a dynamic and vibrant marketplace, where individuals have the opportunity to succeed based on their merits and abilities.

Capitalism also promotes political freedom by decentralizing power and dispersing decision-making authority. In capitalist societies, individuals have the freedom to participate in political processes, express their opinions, and advocate for change. The separation of economic and political spheres ensures that individuals are not subject to arbitrary government control or coercion, safeguarding their civil liberties and rights.

Furthermore, capitalism promotes social freedom by fostering diversity, tolerance, and inclusivity. In capitalist societies, individuals are free to pursue their own cultural, religious, and social identities, without fear of persecution or discrimination. The marketplace of ideas allows for the exchange of diverse perspectives and viewpoints, enriching society and promoting intellectual discourse. Additionally, capitalism provides opportunities for social mobility, allowing individuals to transcend socioeconomic barriers and achieve upward mobility through hard work and determination.

Individual freedom in capitalism extends beyond economic and political realms to encompass personal autonomy and self-expression. In capitalist societies, individuals have the freedom to pursue their own interests, passions, and aspirations, whether it be in the arts, sciences, or leisure activities. This freedom allows individuals to lead fulfilling and meaningful lives, guided by their own values and aspirations.

Moreover, capitalism empowers individuals to take control of their own destinies and shape their own futures. Entrepreneurship, a cornerstone of capitalism, enables individuals to pursue their dreams, create value, and make a positive impact on society. Whether it be starting a small business, launching a tech startup, or inventing a new product, entrepreneurship offers individuals the opportunity to exercise their creativity, initiative, and ingenuity.

Capitalism also promotes individual responsibility and accountability, emphasizing the importance of personal agency and self-reliance. In capitalist societies, individuals are expected to take ownership of their decisions, actions, and outcomes, recognizing that they bear the consequences of their choices. This ethos of personal responsibility fosters a culture of resilience, adaptability, and self-improvement, empowering individuals to overcome challenges and achieve success.

Furthermore, capitalism respects the autonomy of individuals to pursue their own conception of the good life, free from external coercion or imposition. In capitalist societies, individuals have the freedom to make choices about their lifestyles, values, and priorities, whether it be pursuing material wealth, personal fulfillment, or social justice. This diversity of lifestyles and aspirations enriches society and fosters a culture of tolerance, pluralism, and respect for individual differences.

In a nutshell, individual freedom lies at the heart of the case for capitalism, embodying the principle that individuals possess inherent rights and liberties that must be protected and upheld. Capitalism promotes individual freedom by safeguarding property rights, fostering economic and political freedom, promoting social diversity and inclusion, empowering entrepreneurship, and respecting personal autonomy and self-expression. As a system grounded in the principles of liberty, capitalism offers individuals the opportunity to lead autonomous, fulfilling, and meaningful lives, guided by their own values, aspirations, and choices.

Chapter 3: Capitalism in Practice

Capitalism in practice refers to the economic and social system characterized by private ownership of the means of production, free market competition, and minimal government intervention in economic affairs. Capitalism can take various forms and may coexist with different degrees of government regulation and social welfare programs.

Market Mechanisms

In capitalist economies, market mechanisms are the cornerstone of resource allocation, price determination, and economic coordination. These mechanisms operate within the framework of free markets, where supply and demand interact to determine prices and quantities of goods and services exchanged. Market mechanisms rely on the principles of competition, self-interest, and voluntary exchange to ensure efficient allocation of resources and optimal outcomes for producers and consumers alike.

At the heart of market mechanisms lies the concept of supply and demand. Suppliers offer goods and services in response to consumer demand, while consumers express their preferences through their purchasing decisions. The interaction of supply and demand sets equilibrium prices and quantities in markets, reflecting the balance of supply and demand forces. When demand exceeds supply, prices rise, signaling producers to increase output to meet consumer needs. Conversely, when supply exceeds demand, prices fall, signaling producers to reduce output to avoid surpluses.

Price signals play a crucial role in guiding resource allocation within market mechanisms. Prices convey information about relative scarcity, demand, and value, guiding producers and consumers in their decision-making processes. When prices rise, it indicates scarcity or high demand, encouraging producers to allocate more resources towards the production of that good or service. Conversely, when prices fall, it signals abundance or low demand, prompting producers to reallocate resources to more profitable ventures.

Market mechanisms also promote competition among producers, driving efficiency, innovation, and productivity gains. In competitive markets, firms vie for market share by offering better products, services, or prices than their rivals. This competitive pressure incentivizes firms to minimize costs, improve quality, and innovate to gain a competitive edge. As a result, consumers benefit from lower prices, higher quality products, and a wider range of choices in the marketplace.

Moreover, market mechanisms foster consumer sovereignty, allowing individuals to make choices based on their preferences, needs, and budget constraints. Consumers have the freedom to choose among a variety of goods and services offered in the marketplace, influencing production decisions and driving innovation. Producers respond to consumer demand by adjusting their offerings to meet changing preferences, ensuring that resources are allocated in accordance with consumer preferences.

Price flexibility is another hallmark of market mechanisms, enabling prices to adjust freely in response to changes in supply and demand conditions. Flexible prices ensure that markets can reach equilibrium efficiently, minimizing shortages or surpluses and promoting economic efficiency. When prices are allowed to fluctuate, markets can clear quickly, ensuring that resources are allocated to their most valued uses.

Additionally, market mechanisms facilitate the process of market clearing, where supply equals demand and equilibrium is achieved. Market clearing ensures that there are no shortages or surpluses of goods or services, and resources are allocated efficiently. Prices adjust to ensure that supply and demand are in balance, leading to optimal outcomes for producers and consumers.

Arbitrage is another important aspect of market mechanisms, allowing individuals to exploit price differences in different markets to make a profit. Arbitrageurs buy low and sell high, equalizing prices across markets and ensuring that goods and services are priced consistently. Arbitrageurs play a vital role in promoting market efficiency by eliminating price discrepancies and restoring equilibrium in markets.

Furthermore, market mechanisms operate within different market structures, each with its own characteristics that influence market outcomes. Perfectly competitive markets feature many small firms competing for market share, while monopolistic or oligopolistic markets have fewer firms with market power. Market structures affect the behavior of firms and the efficiency of resource allocation within markets.

Externalities and information asymmetry are important considerations within market mechanisms. Externalities are unintended side effects of economic activities that affect third parties, while information asymmetry occurs when one party in a transaction has more information than the other party. Externalities and information asymmetry can lead to market inefficiencies and suboptimal outcomes, necessitating government intervention to correct market failures and ensure efficient resource allocation.

Market mechanisms are essential components of capitalism, facilitating the efficient allocation of resources, price determination, and economic coordination within market economies. By relying on the principles of supply and demand, price signals, competition, and consumer sovereignty, market mechanisms promote efficiency, innovation, and prosperity in capitalist societies. However, market mechanisms are not without limitations, and government intervention may be necessary to address market failures and ensure that markets function in the best interest of society as a whole.

Role of Government

In capitalist societies, the role of government is multifaceted, encompassing various functions aimed at maintaining economic stability, promoting competition, safeguarding public welfare, and addressing market failures. While capitalism emphasizes free markets and minimal government intervention in economic affairs, governments play a crucial role in providing essential public goods and services, regulating markets, enforcing laws, and addressing societal challenges.

One of the primary roles of government in capitalism is to establish and enforce the rule of law. Governments enact laws and regulations that define property rights, contract enforcement, and dispute resolution mechanisms, providing a stable and predictable legal framework for economic activities. The rule of law ensures that individuals and businesses can engage in transactions with confidence, knowing that their rights and obligations are protected by law.

Government also plays a vital role in providing public goods and services that are not efficiently provided by the private sector. Public goods, such as national defense, infrastructure, and public education, exhibit non-excludable and non-rivalrous characteristics, making it difficult for the private sector to supply them efficiently. Governments finance and provide public goods to ensure that all members of society have access to essential services and infrastructure.

Moreover, governments regulate markets to ensure fair competition, consumer protection, and environmental sustainability. Regulatory agencies set and enforce standards for product safety, environmental protection, and workplace conditions, safeguarding public health and safety. Antitrust laws and competition policies prevent monopolistic practices and promote market competition, ensuring that markets remain open and competitive.

In addition to regulation, governments may intervene in markets to address market failures and externalities. Market failures occur when markets fail to allocate resources efficiently due to factors such as externalities, public goods, or imperfect information. Governments may intervene through taxes, subsidies, or regulations to internalize externalities, correct market failures, and promote social welfare.

Furthermore, governments play a crucial role in stabilizing the economy and mitigating economic fluctuations. During periods of recession or economic downturns, governments may implement fiscal and monetary policies to stimulate aggregate demand, promote investment, and create jobs. Conversely, during periods of inflation or overheating, governments may implement contractionary policies to curb inflationary pressures and prevent economic overheating.

Governments also provide social safety nets and welfare programs to support vulnerable populations and reduce income inequality. Social welfare programs, such as unemployment insurance, healthcare, and social assistance, provide financial support to individuals and families facing hardship. By ensuring a basic standard of living for all citizens, welfare programs promote social cohesion and reduce poverty.

Furthermore, governments invest in education and human capital development to enhance productivity, innovation, and economic growth. Public education systems provide access to quality education and training opportunities, equipping individuals with the skills and knowledge needed to succeed in the workforce. Investments in research and development, infrastructure, and technology also contribute to long-term economic growth and competitiveness.

Moreover, governments play a critical role in promoting sustainable development and environmental protection. Environmental regulations and conservation policies aim to mitigate pollution, preserve natural resources, and address climate change. Governments may impose taxes, subsidies, or emissions trading schemes to incentivize businesses to reduce their environmental impact and adopt cleaner technologies.

In times of crisis or emergency, governments serve as providers of last resort, stepping in to address urgent needs and ensure public safety. During natural disasters, pandemics, or other emergencies, governments coordinate disaster response efforts, provide emergency services, and mobilize resources to support affected communities.

Additionally, governments engage in diplomacy, trade negotiations, and international cooperation to promote economic growth, peace, and stability on the global stage. By participating in international organizations and agreements, governments facilitate trade, investment, and economic development, benefiting both domestic and global economies.

However, government intervention in capitalist economies is not without challenges and controversies. Excessive regulation and bureaucracy can stifle innovation, entrepreneurship, and economic growth, hindering the dynamism of free markets. Moreover, government interventions may be subject to political influence, rent-seeking behavior, and inefficiencies, undermining their effectiveness and legitimacy.

In summary, the role of government in capitalism is multifaceted, encompassing functions such as establishing the rule of law, providing public goods and services, regulating markets, addressing market failures, stabilizing the economy, promoting social welfare, and safeguarding public safety and the environment. While capitalism emphasizes free markets and minimal government intervention, governments play a crucial role in ensuring economic stability, promoting social cohesion, and addressing societal challenges in capitalist societies.

Regulation and Deregulation

Regulation and deregulation are central themes in the implementation of capitalism, shaping the balance between government intervention and market freedom. Regulation refers to the imposition of rules, standards, and restrictions by government authorities to govern economic activities, ensure public welfare, and address market failures. Deregulation, on the other hand, involves the removal or relaxation of regulations and restrictions, aiming to promote competition, efficiency, and innovation in markets.

Regulation serves various purposes in capitalist economies, including protecting consumers, safeguarding public health and safety, and promoting environmental sustainability. Consumer protection regulations, such as product safety standards and truth in advertising laws, ensure that consumers are not misled or harmed by deceptive practices. Health and safety regulations set standards for workplace conditions, food safety, and pharmaceuticals, reducing risks to public health and safety. Environmental regulations aim to mitigate pollution, conserve natural resources, and address climate change, promoting sustainable development and environmental stewardship.

Moreover, regulation plays a crucial role in promoting fair competition and preventing monopolistic practices in markets. Antitrust laws and competition policies prohibit anti-competitive behavior, such as price-fixing, market allocation, and monopolization, ensuring that markets remain open, competitive, and conducive to innovation. Regulatory agencies enforce competition laws, investigate anti-competitive conduct, and impose penalties on violators, maintaining a level playing field for businesses and protecting consumer welfare.

Regulation also provides stability and predictability in markets, reducing uncertainty and systemic risks. Financial regulations, such as capital requirements, risk management standards, and disclosure requirements, aim to promote financial stability and prevent systemic crises. Regulatory oversight of financial institutions, such as banks, insurance companies, and securities firms, helps mitigate risks and prevent market failures that could have far-reaching consequences for the economy.

Additionally, regulation can address market failures and externalities that arise from imperfect information, incomplete markets, or public goods. Government intervention may be necessary to internalize externalities, correct market distortions, and promote social welfare. For example, taxes on pollution or subsidies for renewable energy aim to incentivize environmentally friendly behavior and reduce negative externalities associated with pollution.

However, regulation is not without drawbacks and limitations. Excessive or poorly designed regulations can stifle innovation, entrepreneurship, and economic growth, imposing compliance costs and administrative burdens on businesses. Regulatory capture, where regulatory agencies are influenced by industry interests or lobbying groups, can lead to regulations that serve special interests rather than the public good. Moreover, regulatory complexity and inconsistency can create barriers to entry, disadvantage small businesses, and hinder market competition.

Deregulation, by contrast, aims to promote market efficiency, competition, and innovation by removing unnecessary regulations and bureaucratic barriers. Deregulatory efforts seek to streamline regulatory processes, reduce compliance costs, and enhance regulatory flexibility, allowing businesses to operate more efficiently and adapt to changing market conditions. Deregulation can stimulate economic growth, create jobs, and foster entrepreneurship by freeing businesses from burdensome regulations and promoting market dynamism.

Moreover, deregulation can lead to increased competition and lower prices for consumers by removing barriers to entry and encouraging market entry. In deregulated industries such as telecommunications, energy, and transportation, competition has increased, leading to greater choice, lower prices, and improved quality of services for consumers. Deregulation can also spur innovation and technological advancement by fostering a more competitive and dynamic market environment.

However, deregulation is not without risks and challenges. Removing regulations intended to protect public health, safety, and the environment can expose consumers to risks and vulnerabilities. Deregulation may lead to market concentration, where a few large firms dominate the market and wield significant market power, reducing competition and consumer choice. Moreover, deregulation can exacerbate income inequality and social disparities by favoring large corporations and wealthy individuals at the expense of small businesses and vulnerable populations.

Furthermore, deregulation can contribute to market instability and systemic risks, particularly in financial markets. Relaxing regulations on financial institutions and markets can increase the likelihood of speculative bubbles, excessive risk-taking, and financial crises. The 2008 global financial crisis, which was precipitated by deregulation and lax oversight in the financial sector, underscored the risks of deregulatory approaches and the importance of prudent regulation in safeguarding financial stability.

In summary, regulation and deregulation are essential elements of capitalist economies, shaping the balance between government intervention and market freedom. Regulation plays a crucial role in protecting consumers, safeguarding public welfare, and promoting market competition, while deregulation aims to promote efficiency, innovation, and competition by removing unnecessary regulations and bureaucratic barriers. However, both regulation and deregulation carry risks and trade-offs, and policymakers must carefully weigh the benefits and drawbacks of regulatory interventions to ensure that markets function in the best interest of society as a whole.

Chapter 4: The Moral Dimension

The moral dimension of capitalism is a topic of significant debate and discussion, encompassing questions about justice, fairness, and ethical behavior within the context of economic systems based on private ownership, free markets, and profit maximization. While capitalism has been praised for its ability to generate wealth, promote innovation, and raise living standards, it has also faced criticism for exacerbating inequalities, fostering exploitation, and prioritizing profits over human welfare.

One of the central moral arguments in favor of capitalism is its emphasis on individual freedom and autonomy. Capitalism champions the principles of personal liberty, private property rights, and voluntary exchange, allowing individuals to pursue their own interests, make choices based on their preferences, and engage in economic activities without coercion or interference. From a moral perspective, capitalism upholds the dignity and autonomy of individuals, recognizing their right to self-determination and economic independence.

Capitalism and Ethics

The relationship between capitalism and ethics is a subject of ongoing debate and inquiry, exploring the moral dimensions of economic systems based on private ownership, free markets, and profit-seeking behavior. While capitalism has been praised for its ability to generate wealth, promote innovation, and improve living standards, it has also faced criticism for exacerbating inequalities, fostering exploitation, and prioritizing profits over ethical considerations.

One of the central ethical principles underlying capitalism is the concept of individual freedom and autonomy. Capitalism champions the principles of personal liberty, property rights, and voluntary exchange, emphasizing individuals' rights to make choices, pursue their own interests, and engage in economic activities without coercion or interference. From an ethical standpoint, capitalism upholds the dignity and autonomy of individuals, recognizing their right to self-determination and economic independence.

Moreover, capitalism is often associated with the idea of meritocracy, where individuals are rewarded based on their talents, efforts, and contributions to society. In capitalist economies, individuals have the opportunity to succeed through hard work, entrepreneurship, and innovation, regardless of their background or social status. The meritocratic ethos of capitalism aligns with ethical principles of fairness and equality of opportunity, rewarding individuals for their achievements and contributions to society.

Furthermore, capitalism promotes social cooperation, peaceful exchange, and mutual benefit through the mechanism of voluntary exchange. In capitalist markets, individuals and businesses engage in transactions based on mutual consent and agreement, exchanging goods, services, and resources to their mutual advantage. This voluntary exchange fosters economic cooperation, specialization, and division of labor, leading to increased productivity, efficiency, and prosperity.

However, capitalism also raises ethical concerns and moral dilemmas that warrant consideration. One of the most pressing issues is income inequality and wealth concentration, which can undermine social cohesion, exacerbate disparities, and perpetuate systemic injustices. Critics argue that capitalism tends to disproportionately benefit the wealthy and powerful, exacerbating inequalities of income, wealth, and opportunity, and perpetuating social stratification.

Moreover, capitalism has been criticized for fostering exploitation, commodification, and alienation in labor relations. In capitalist economies, labor is treated as a commodity to be bought and sold in the marketplace, leading to wage labor, labor exploitation, and precarious working conditions for many workers. Critics argue that capitalism's focus on profit maximization can lead to exploitation of workers, environmental degradation, and disregard for social welfare.

Additionally, capitalism has been associated with the commodification of goods, services, and even human relationships, where everything is assigned a market value and subjected to market forces. Critics argue that this commodification mentality can erode social values, relationships, and community ties, reducing human interactions to transactions and undermining moral and ethical norms.

Furthermore, capitalism's emphasis on short-term profit maximization and shareholder value has been criticized for prioritizing financial gains over long-term sustainability, environmental stewardship, and social responsibility. Critics argue that capitalism's relentless pursuit of profit can lead to unethical behavior, corporate misconduct, and disregard for ethical considerations in business decisions.

In response to these ethical concerns, proponents of capitalism advocate for policies and practices that promote ethical behavior, social responsibility, and sustainable development within capitalist economies. This includes initiatives such as corporate social responsibility, ethical investing, fair labor practices, environmental sustainability, and social welfare programs aimed at mitigating inequalities and addressing social injustices.

Moreover, capitalism has the potential to contribute positively to ethical outcomes by fostering economic growth, innovation, and human flourishing. Capitalism has lifted millions of people out of poverty, provided opportunities for upward mobility, and improved living standards on a global scale. From an ethical perspective, capitalism's ability to generate wealth and prosperity contributes to human well-being and societal advancement.

However, it is essential to recognize that capitalism is not inherently ethical or unethical; rather, its ethical implications depend on how it is practiced and regulated within a given society. Governments, policymakers, businesses, and individuals all have a role to play in shaping the ethical dimensions of capitalism and ensuring that economic systems prioritize human welfare, social justice, and environmental sustainability.

In conclusion, the relationship between capitalism and ethics is complex and multifaceted, encompassing a range of moral considerations related to justice, fairness, and human welfare. While capitalism has the potential to promote individual freedom, economic prosperity, and social cooperation, it also raises ethical concerns about inequality, exploitation, and commodification. Addressing these ethical challenges requires a nuanced approach that balances economic freedom with ethical considerations, promoting social responsibility, fairness, and human dignity within capitalist economies.

Social Responsibility

Within the moral dimension of capitalism, the concept of social responsibility holds significant importance. Social responsibility refers to the ethical obligation of individuals and organizations to act in ways that benefit society, beyond their narrow economic interests. In the context of capitalism, social responsibility addresses the broader impact of economic activities on communities, stakeholders, and the environment, emphasizing ethical behavior, sustainability, and concern for the welfare of others.

One aspect of social responsibility in capitalism involves ethical business practices and corporate behavior. Businesses are expected to adhere to ethical standards, respect human rights, and uphold principles of fairness, integrity, and transparency in their operations. This includes treating employees fairly, providing safe working conditions, and respecting labor rights, as well as engaging in ethical sourcing, production, and marketing practices.

Moreover, social responsibility encompasses environmental sustainability and stewardship. Businesses have a responsibility to minimize their environmental footprint, reduce pollution, conserve natural resources, and mitigate climate change. This may involve adopting eco-friendly practices, investing in renewable energy, reducing waste, and incorporating sustainable technologies and processes into their operations.

Furthermore, social responsibility extends to corporate philanthropy, community engagement, and social investment. Businesses are encouraged to contribute to the well-being of society by supporting charitable causes, community development initiatives, and social welfare programs. This may include donating to charities, volunteering time and resources, and investing in projects that address social needs, such as education, healthcare, poverty alleviation, and infrastructure development.

Additionally, social responsibility involves ethical investment and financial practices. Investors and financial institutions are increasingly considering environmental, social, and governance (ESG) factors in their investment decisions, seeking to align their investments with ethical and sustainable principles. This may involve divesting from companies with poor social or environmental records and investing in companies that demonstrate strong ethical practices and positive social impact.

Moreover, social responsibility extends to government and public policy, as policymakers have a responsibility to enact laws and regulations that promote social welfare, environmental sustainability, and economic justice. Governments play a crucial role in regulating markets, enforcing labor and environmental standards, protecting consumers, and addressing social inequalities through policies such as taxation, social welfare programs, and environmental regulations.

Furthermore, social responsibility encompasses individual actions and choices, as individuals have a moral obligation to contribute to the well-being of society and the environment. This may involve volunteering, charitable giving, ethical consumption, and advocacy for social and environmental causes. Individuals can support businesses that demonstrate ethical behavior and sustainability practices, and hold companies accountable for their social and environmental impact through consumer activism and social media advocacy.

Social responsibility is an integral aspect of capitalism, addressing the ethical obligations of individuals, businesses, and governments to promote the well-being of society and the environment. By embracing social responsibility, businesses can enhance their reputation, build trust with stakeholders, and create long-term value for shareholders. Moreover, social responsibility fosters a more sustainable and equitable form of capitalism, promoting economic prosperity, social justice, and environmental sustainability for present and future generations.

Wealth Distribution

Within the moral dimension of capitalism, wealth distribution is a critical aspect that raises ethical considerations about fairness, justice, and societal well-being. Capitalism, as an economic system, is characterized by the private ownership of resources and the pursuit of profit, which can lead to disparities in wealth and income distribution. Addressing wealth distribution within capitalism requires a nuanced understanding of the factors that contribute to inequality and the moral implications of these disparities.

One of the primary ethical concerns surrounding wealth distribution in capitalism is income inequality. Capitalist economies often exhibit significant disparities in income, with some individuals and groups accruing vast amounts of wealth while others struggle to meet their basic needs. This unequal distribution of income can lead to social unrest, undermine social cohesion, and perpetuate systemic injustices, posing moral challenges for society.

Moreover, wealth inequality in capitalism can exacerbate disparities in opportunity, limiting social mobility and perpetuating intergenerational poverty. Individuals born into disadvantaged socioeconomic backgrounds may face barriers to accessing education, healthcare, and economic opportunities, further entrenching inequality and limiting their prospects for upward mobility. From a moral perspective, ensuring equal opportunity and social mobility is essential for promoting fairness and justice within capitalist societies.

Furthermore, wealth distribution in capitalism can impact political power dynamics and influence policymaking processes. Individuals and corporations with significant wealth and resources may wield disproportionate influence over political decision-making, shaping policies to benefit their interests at the expense of the broader public good. This concentration of economic and political power raises concerns about democratic governance, accountability, and representation within capitalist societies.

Additionally, the concentration of wealth in the hands of a few individuals or entities can have adverse effects on economic stability and resilience. When wealth is highly concentrated, it can lead to economic fragility, speculative bubbles, and financial crises, as seen in historical examples such as the Great Depression and the 2008 global financial crisis. Addressing wealth concentration is essential for promoting economic stability, reducing systemic risks, and safeguarding the well-being of society as a whole.

Moreover, wealth distribution within capitalism raises questions about the moral legitimacy of property rights and the distribution of resources. While capitalism upholds the right to private property and individual ownership, disparities in wealth distribution may call into question the fairness of these property rights, especially when wealth is inherited or accumulated through exploitation, rent-seeking behavior, or unethical practices. From a moral perspective, ensuring that property rights are based on principles of justice, fairness, and social utility is essential for promoting a just and equitable society.

In response to these moral concerns, various approaches have been proposed to address wealth distribution within capitalism. Progressive taxation, for example, seeks to redistribute wealth and income from the affluent to the less affluent through a system of taxation that imposes higher tax rates on higher incomes. Wealth redistribution programs, such as social welfare programs, unemployment benefits, and progressive income taxes, aim to mitigate poverty, reduce inequality, and promote social welfare.

Moreover, policies aimed at increasing access to education, healthcare, and economic opportunities can help level the playing field and promote equal opportunity within capitalist societies. Investing in education and skills development, providing affordable healthcare and social services, and implementing affirmative action and anti-discrimination policies can help address structural barriers to social mobility and promote a more equitable distribution of wealth and opportunity.

Furthermore, promoting ethical business practices, corporate social responsibility, and sustainable development can help mitigate wealth disparities and promote shared prosperity within capitalist economies. Businesses have a responsibility to consider the broader social and environmental impact of their operations, engage with stakeholders, and contribute to the well-being of society through ethical conduct, philanthropy, and sustainable business practices.

Wealth distribution is a central ethical concern within capitalism, raising questions about fairness, justice, and societal well-being. Addressing wealth distribution requires a multifaceted approach that considers the root causes of inequality, the moral implications of wealth disparities, and the potential solutions for promoting a more just and equitable society. By promoting policies and practices that foster economic opportunity, social mobility, and shared prosperity, capitalist societies can work towards creating a more inclusive and sustainable future for all.

Chapter 5: Challenges and Criticisms

Capitalism, as an economic system based on private ownership of the means of production and the pursuit of profit, has faced numerous challenges and criticisms throughout its history. While capitalism has been praised for its ability to generate wealth, promote innovation, and improve living standards, it has also been subject to scrutiny and debate regarding its social, economic, and environmental impacts.

Inequality

Inequality stands as one of the most pronounced criticisms of capitalism, as it often generates significant disparities in wealth, income, and opportunity within societies. Capitalism's emphasis on individual initiative, competition, and profit maximization can exacerbate inequality through various mechanisms, leading to social unrest, economic inefficiency, and moral dilemmas.

One of the primary drivers of inequality in capitalist societies is the unequal distribution of income. Capitalism allows individuals and businesses to accumulate wealth through ownership of capital, entrepreneurship, and investment. However, this can result in a concentration of income and wealth among a small segment of the population, while leaving many others struggling to make ends meet.

Moreover, capitalism's reliance on market forces and competition can lead to wage disparities between different sectors, occupations, and skill levels. High-skilled workers in industries such as technology and finance often command higher salaries and benefits, while low-skilled workers in sectors like retail and hospitality may earn minimum wages with limited job security and benefits. This wage gap contributes to income inequality and social stratification within capitalist economies.

Additionally, capitalism's emphasis on profit maximization can lead to exploitation of labor, particularly in industries with low barriers to entry and limited worker protections. Employers may engage in practices such as wage theft, unpaid overtime, and unsafe working conditions to maximize profits, leaving workers vulnerable to exploitation and abuse. This exploitation can exacerbate income inequality and perpetuate cycles of poverty and disadvantage.

Furthermore, capitalism's reliance on private ownership of property and capital can lead to wealth concentration among a small elite, as those with access to capital can accumulate wealth more easily than those without. This concentration of wealth can lead to the perpetuation of intergenerational inequality, as wealth is passed down through inheritance, perpetuating privilege and disadvantage across generations.

Moreover, capitalism's focus on shareholder value and short-term profit maximization can lead to corporate practices that prioritize the interests of shareholders over those of workers, communities, and the environment. This can result in wage stagnation, job loss, and environmental degradation, exacerbating inequality and social dislocation within capitalist economies.

Additionally, capitalism's reliance on competition and market forces can lead to winner-takes-all outcomes, where a small number of individuals or companies capture a disproportionate share of wealth and resources. This can create monopolies, oligopolies, and market distortions that further exacerbate inequality and limit opportunities for smaller businesses and individuals.

Moreover, capitalism's emphasis on consumerism and materialism can exacerbate inequality by creating a culture of conspicuous consumption and status competition. Those with greater wealth and purchasing power can afford to consume luxury goods and services, while others struggle to meet their basic needs. This consumption gap can contribute to social stratification and reinforce patterns of inequality within capitalist societies.

Furthermore, capitalism's reliance on financial markets and speculative investment can lead to asset bubbles and financial instability, exacerbating inequality and volatility within economies. Financial crises, such as the 2008 global financial crisis, often have disproportionate impacts on low-income households, exacerbating inequality and widening the wealth gap.

Additionally, capitalism's reliance on technological innovation and automation can lead to job displacement and income inequality, as automation replaces labor in various industries. While technological advancements can lead to increased productivity and economic growth, they can also contribute to job polarization and wage inequality, leaving many workers behind.

Moreover, capitalism's global nature can exacerbate inequality on a global scale, as wealthy nations and multinational corporations often benefit disproportionately from global trade and investment, while developing countries and marginalized communities bear the brunt of exploitation and environmental degradation. This global inequality can perpetuate cycles of poverty and disadvantage, widening the gap between rich and poor countries.

Inequality stands as a central challenge and criticism of capitalism, as it often generates significant disparities in wealth, income, and opportunity within societies. Addressing inequality requires comprehensive policies and interventions that promote social justice, economic opportunity, and shared prosperity within capitalist economies. By addressing the root causes of inequality and promoting inclusive growth and development, societies can work towards building more equitable and sustainable economies that benefit all members of society.

Environmental Impact

The environmental impact of capitalism is a significant concern, as the pursuit of profit and economic growth often comes at the expense of environmental sustainability and ecological health. Capitalism's reliance on resource extraction, industrial production, and consumerism has led to widespread environmental degradation, pollution, and climate change, posing significant challenges for ecosystems, biodiversity, and human well-being.

One of the primary environmental criticisms of capitalism is its reliance on fossil fuels and other non-renewable resources for energy production and industrial activities. The burning of fossil fuels, such as coal, oil, and natural gas, releases greenhouse gases into the atmosphere, contributing to global warming and climate change. Moreover, fossil fuel extraction and combustion lead to air and water pollution, ecosystem degradation, and adverse health impacts for communities living near extraction sites and industrial facilities.

Additionally, capitalism's emphasis on economic growth and consumption has led to unsustainable levels of resource extraction, depletion, and waste generation. The linear model of production and consumption, known as the "take-make-waste" model, results in the extraction of raw materials, production of goods, and disposal of waste, leading to resource depletion, pollution, and environmental degradation. This unsustainable use of resources undermines the long-term viability of ecosystems and threatens the stability of Earth's natural systems.

Furthermore, capitalism's reliance on industrial agriculture and intensive farming practices has led to deforestation, habitat destruction, and loss of biodiversity. Large-scale monoculture farming, use of chemical fertilizers and pesticides, and expansion of agricultural land into natural habitats have resulted in the destruction of forests, wetlands, and other ecosystems, leading to loss of biodiversity and degradation of soil and water resources.

Moreover, capitalism's emphasis on economic growth and profit maximization often comes at the expense of environmental conservation and protection. Short-term economic interests may prioritize resource extraction, pollution, and environmental degradation over long-term sustainability and ecological health. This "tragedy of the commons" mentality can lead to overexploitation of natural resources and degradation of shared environmental resources, undermining the well-being of present and future generations.

Additionally, capitalism's reliance on consumerism and planned obsolescence has led to the production of disposable, single-use products and packaging, contributing to waste generation and pollution. The proliferation of plastic waste, electronic waste, and other non-biodegradable materials has resulted in pollution of land, water, and air, posing threats to wildlife, ecosystems, and human health.

Furthermore, capitalism's emphasis on economic growth and expansion has led to urbanization, sprawl, and land development, resulting in habitat destruction, fragmentation, and loss of open spaces. Urbanization and development often encroach upon natural habitats, disrupt ecological processes, and displace wildlife, leading to biodiversity loss and ecological imbalance.

Moreover, capitalism's global nature has led to environmental exploitation and degradation in developing countries, as multinational corporations seek to maximize profits by exploiting cheap labor, lax environmental regulations, and natural resources in these regions. This neocolonialist approach to resource extraction and production often leads to environmental destruction, social injustice, and human rights abuses in host countries.

Additionally, capitalism's reliance on growth-driven economic models has led to a culture of overconsumption and waste, where individuals and societies prioritize material wealth and consumption over environmental sustainability and quality of life. This culture of consumerism contributes to resource depletion, pollution, and environmental degradation, perpetuating unsustainable patterns of production and consumption.

Moreover, capitalism's emphasis on economic competition and market forces can hinder collective action and cooperation needed to address environmental challenges such as climate change, pollution, and biodiversity loss. The pursuit of profit and self-interest may lead businesses and governments to prioritize short-term economic gains over long-term environmental sustainability, undermining efforts to mitigate and adapt to environmental threats.

Furthermore, capitalism's reliance on growth-driven economic models may perpetuate the notion of perpetual growth and expansion, leading to unsustainable levels of consumption, production, and waste generation. This growth-centric mindset fails to account for environmental limits and planetary boundaries, leading to overshoot and ecological collapse.

The environmental impact of capitalism is a significant challenge and criticism, as the pursuit of profit and economic growth often comes at the expense of environmental sustainability and ecological health. Addressing these environmental challenges requires a fundamental rethinking of capitalism's relationship with the environment, as well as transformative changes in economic systems, policies, and behaviors to prioritize environmental conservation, protection, and sustainability. By adopting a more holistic and sustainable approach to economic development, societies can work towards building resilient, equitable, and environmentally sustainable economies that benefit both people and the planet.

Globalization

Globalization, while often seen as a key aspect of capitalist economies, is also a source of significant criticism and challenge. Globalization refers to the increasing interconnectedness and interdependence of economies, cultures, and societies through trade, investment, technology, and information exchange. While globalization has brought about economic growth, technological advancement, and cultural exchange, it has also raised concerns about inequality, exploitation, and cultural homogenization.

One of the primary criticisms of globalization is its role in exacerbating economic inequality both within and between countries. Globalization has led to the concentration of wealth and power in the hands of a few multinational corporations and wealthy individuals, while leaving many workers and communities behind. The globalization of trade and investment has enabled companies to move production to countries with lower labor costs and weaker labor protections, leading to job displacement, wage stagnation, and widening income inequality in many countries.

Moreover, globalization has been criticized for its impact on labor rights and working conditions, particularly in developing countries where labor standards may be weaker and enforcement may be lacking. Globalization has enabled companies to outsource production to countries with lax labor regulations and lower wages, leading to exploitation of workers, unsafe working conditions, and violations of labor rights. This race to the bottom in labor standards has contributed to a race to the bottom in wages and working conditions, exacerbating inequality and social injustice.

Additionally, globalization has been accused of exacerbating environmental degradation and ecological destruction, as companies seek to exploit natural resources and externalize environmental costs in pursuit of profit. The globalization of production and consumption has led to increased resource extraction, pollution, and habitat destruction, posing significant threats to ecosystems, biodiversity, and planetary health. Moreover, the transportation of goods and people across borders has contributed to carbon emissions, air pollution, and climate change, exacerbating environmental challenges on a global scale.

Furthermore, globalization has raised concerns about cultural homogenization and the erosion of cultural diversity and identity. The spread of global brands, media, and consumer culture has led to the dominance of Western cultural norms and values at the expense of local traditions, languages, and customs. This cultural homogenization can undermine cultural diversity, cultural heritage, and social cohesion, leading to a loss of identity and sense of belonging for many communities.

Moreover, globalization has been criticized for its impact on democracy and sovereignty, as global economic integration and interconnectedness can undermine the ability of governments to regulate markets, protect citizens, and pursue social and environmental goals. The rise of global trade agreements, multinational corporations, and supranational organizations has shifted power away from democratic institutions and towards unelected bodies and corporate interests, raising concerns about democratic governance, accountability, and representation.

Additionally, globalization has been accused of exacerbating financial instability and volatility, as global capital flows and speculative investment can lead to currency crises, financial contagion, and economic crises. The interconnectedness of global financial markets and the proliferation of complex financial instruments have made economies more vulnerable to external shocks and speculative bubbles, posing risks to financial stability and economic prosperity.

Furthermore, globalization has been criticized for its uneven distribution of benefits and costs, as some countries and social groups benefit disproportionately from globalization while others bear the brunt of its negative consequences. Developing countries and marginalized communities often lack the resources, infrastructure, and institutions to fully participate in global markets and benefit from globalization, leading to widening disparities in income, wealth, and opportunity.

Moreover, globalization has been accused of exacerbating social and political instability, as economic dislocation, cultural change, and social upheaval can fuel resentment, conflict, and extremism. The globalization of trade and investment has led to the displacement of traditional industries and livelihoods, as well as the erosion of social safety nets and community cohesion, leading to social tensions and political polarization.

Furthermore, globalization has raised concerns about food security and sovereignty, as global trade and supply chains can disrupt local food systems and undermine food sovereignty. The globalization of agriculture and food production has led to increased reliance on monoculture crops, chemical inputs, and genetically modified organisms, posing risks to biodiversity, soil health, and food security. Moreover, global trade agreements and corporate consolidation in the food industry have marginalized small-scale farmers and local food producers, threatening food sovereignty and local food cultures.

While globalization has brought about economic growth, technological advancement, and cultural exchange, it has also raised significant challenges and criticisms. From exacerbating economic inequality and environmental degradation to undermining cultural diversity and sovereignty, globalization poses complex and multifaceted challenges that require careful consideration and response. Addressing the challenges of globalization requires efforts to promote inclusive and sustainable development, protect human rights and labor standards, and strengthen democratic governance and social cohesion in a globalized world.

Chapter 6: The Future of Capitalism

Predicting the future of capitalism is a complex task, as it is influenced by a myriad of economic, social, technological, and political factors. However, several trends and developments suggest potential directions for the future evolution of capitalism.

One key trend shaping the future of capitalism is the increasing focus on sustainability and social responsibility. As awareness of environmental and social issues grows, there is a growing recognition that capitalism must evolve to address these challenges. This includes efforts to integrate environmental, social, and governance (ESG) factors into business practices, investment decisions, and policymaking processes. Companies are increasingly adopting sustainable business practices, investing in renewable energy, reducing waste, and addressing social inequalities. Moreover, consumers and investors are demanding greater transparency, accountability, and ethical behavior from businesses, leading to a shift towards more responsible capitalism.

Adapting to Change

Adapting to change is a fundamental aspect of the future of capitalism, as the economic system navigates through a rapidly evolving global landscape shaped by technological advancements, demographic shifts, environmental challenges, and geopolitical dynamics. Adapting to change in the context of capitalism involves embracing innovation, flexibility, and resilience to address emerging challenges and seize new opportunities.

One key aspect of adapting to change in capitalism is fostering innovation and entrepreneurship. Innovation drives economic growth, creates new industries and job opportunities, and enhances productivity and competitiveness. The future of capitalism will likely see increased investment in research and development, technology adoption, and innovation ecosystems to spur creativity, entrepreneurship, and technological advancement. Governments, businesses, and educational institutions will need to collaborate to create supportive environments for innovation, providing funding, infrastructure, and incentives for startups, small businesses, and research institutions to develop and commercialize new ideas and technologies.

It involves embracing technological advancements and digital transformation. Digitalization is reshaping industries, business models, and consumer behavior, creating new opportunities for efficiency, connectivity, and innovation. The future of capitalism will likely see increased reliance on digital technologies such as artificial intelligence, automation, blockchain, and the Internet of Things to streamline processes, enhance decision-making, and improve customer experiences. Businesses will need to invest in digital infrastructure, talent, and capabilities to remain competitive in an increasingly digital world.

Furthermore, adapting to change in capitalism requires addressing environmental challenges and promoting sustainability. Climate change, resource depletion, and environmental degradation pose significant risks to economic stability, social welfare, and planetary health. The future of capitalism will likely see increased emphasis on sustainable development, renewable energy, and circular economy principles to reduce carbon emissions, conserve natural resources, and mitigate environmental impacts. Businesses will need to adopt sustainable business practices, invest in clean technologies, and embrace corporate social responsibility to meet evolving consumer expectations and regulatory requirements.

Additionally, it involves addressing social inequalities and promoting inclusive growth. Rising income inequality, demographic shifts, and technological disruptions are exacerbating social tensions and widening disparities within societies. The future of capitalism will likely see increased focus on social justice, equity, and inclusion, with efforts to create opportunities for marginalized groups, strengthen social safety nets, and address systemic barriers to economic mobility. Governments, businesses, and civil society will need to collaborate to address social inequalities and promote inclusive economic growth that benefits all members of society.

Moreover, adapting to change in capitalism requires fostering resilience and agility in the face of uncertainty and volatility. Globalization, geopolitical tensions, and technological disruptions are creating new risks and challenges for businesses and economies. The future of capitalism will likely see increased emphasis on risk management, contingency planning, and adaptive governance structures to navigate through turbulent times. Businesses will need to diversify supply chains, build redundancy into critical systems, and embrace agile methodologies to respond quickly to changing market conditions and emerging threats.

Change is essential for the future of capitalism, as the economic system navigates through a rapidly changing global landscape. Embracing innovation, digital transformation, sustainability, and inclusivity will be key to driving economic growth, promoting social welfare, and ensuring environmental sustainability in the years to come. By embracing change and proactively addressing emerging challenges, capitalism can continue to evolve and thrive in the 21st century.

Technological Advances

In discussing the future of capitalism, technological advances play a pivotal role in shaping the trajectory of economic development, productivity, and innovation. As we look ahead, several key technological advancements are likely to have profound impacts on the future of capitalism.

Another important technological advance is the Internet of Things (IoT), which refers to the network of interconnected devices, sensors, and systems that enable the exchange of data and information. The IoT has the potential to transform industries such as healthcare, agriculture, and smart cities by enabling real-time monitoring, analysis, and optimization of systems and processes. In capitalist economies, the IoT can lead to increased efficiency, cost savings, and innovation by enabling businesses to collect and analyze vast amounts of data to inform decision-making and improve operations.

Furthermore, blockchain technology is another technological advance with significant implications for the future of capitalism. Blockchain, a decentralized ledger technology, has the potential to revolutionize industries such as finance, supply chain management, and digital identity verification.

By enabling secure, transparent, and tamper-proof transactions and record-keeping, blockchain can reduce costs, eliminate intermediaries, and increase trust and transparency in capitalist economies. Moreover, blockchain-based cryptocurrencies and digital assets have the potential to disrupt traditional financial systems and democratize access to financial services and capital.

Moreover, advances in biotechnology and genomics are likely to have profound impacts on the future of capitalism, particularly in industries such as healthcare, pharmaceuticals, and agriculture. Breakthroughs in gene editing, personalized medicine, and agricultural biotechnology have the potential to improve human health, enhance crop yields, and address global challenges such as food insecurity and disease. In capitalist economies, biotechnology innovations can lead to new investment opportunities, job creation, and economic growth, as businesses leverage biotech advancements to develop new products and services.

Additionally, renewable energy technologies such as solar, wind, and battery storage are reshaping the future of capitalism by providing cleaner, more sustainable alternatives to fossil fuels. The transition to renewable energy sources has the potential to create new industries, jobs, and investment opportunities while reducing carbon emissions and mitigating climate change. In capitalist economies, renewable energy technologies can drive economic growth, innovation, and competitiveness by reducing energy costs, enhancing energy security, and promoting environmental sustainability.

Furthermore, advances in 3D printing, nanotechnology, and materials science are revolutionizing manufacturing and production processes, enabling businesses to create customized products, reduce waste, and increase efficiency. Additive manufacturing technologies such as 3D printing have the potential to disrupt traditional manufacturing industries by enabling decentralized production, rapid prototyping, and on-demand manufacturing. In capitalist economies, these technologies can lead to new business models, supply chain efficiencies, and economic opportunities.

In a nutshell, technological advances are poised to play a central role in shaping the future of capitalism, driving innovation, productivity, and economic growth. From artificial intelligence and blockchain to renewable energy and biotechnology, these advancements have the potential to transform industries, disrupt traditional business models, and create new opportunities for entrepreneurship and investment. By embracing and harnessing these technological innovations, capitalist economies can continue to evolve and thrive in the 21st century.

Global Perspectives

When discussing the future of capitalism, it's essential to consider global perspectives, as capitalism operates within an interconnected and interdependent global economy. The future of capitalism will be shaped by a variety of global factors, including economic trends, geopolitical dynamics, social movements, and technological advancements.

One key aspect of global perspectives on the future of capitalism is the rise of emerging economies and the shifting balance of economic power. Countries such as China, India, Brazil, and Indonesia are experiencing rapid economic growth and industrialization, driving global demand for goods and services, and reshaping global trade and investment patterns. The future of capitalism will likely see increased economic integration and competition from emerging economies, as they become major players in global markets and supply chains.

Moreover, the future of capitalism will be influenced by geopolitical dynamics and shifts in global governance structures. Rising geopolitical tensions, trade disputes, and regional conflicts can disrupt global trade, investment, and economic cooperation, leading to increased uncertainty and volatility in global markets. Moreover, the future of capitalism may see calls for reform of international institutions such as the World Trade Organization (WTO), International Monetary Fund (IMF), and World Bank to better reflect the changing balance of power and address emerging global challenges such as climate change, pandemics, and cyber threats.

Furthermore, global perspectives on the future of capitalism include considerations of social and environmental sustainability. As awareness of environmental and social issues grows, there is a growing recognition that capitalism must evolve to address these challenges. The future of capitalism will likely see increased emphasis on sustainable development, renewable energy, and circular economy principles to reduce carbon emissions, conserve natural resources, and mitigate environmental impacts. Moreover, there may be increased scrutiny of multinational corporations and global supply chains to ensure that they uphold labor standards, environmental regulations, and human rights.

Additionally, the future of capitalism will be shaped by technological advancements and digital transformation on a global scale. Technological innovations such as artificial intelligence, blockchain, and the Internet of Things have the potential to revolutionize industries, disrupt traditional business models, and create new opportunities for innovation and entrepreneurship. Moreover, the digitalization of economies and societies is enabling greater connectivity, information exchange, and collaboration across borders, leading to increased globalization and economic interdependence.

Furthermore, global perspectives on the future of capitalism include considerations of social inequalities and economic disparities. Rising income inequality, demographic shifts, and technological disruptions are exacerbating social tensions and widening disparities within and between countries. The future of capitalism will likely see increased focus on social justice, equity, and inclusion, with efforts to create opportunities for marginalized groups, strengthen social safety nets, and address systemic barriers to economic mobility. Moreover, there may be calls for reforms to taxation, labor markets, and social welfare systems to ensure that the benefits of capitalism are shared equitably among all members of society.

In conclusion, global perspectives on the future of capitalism encompass a wide range of economic, social, environmental, and technological factors. As capitalism continues to evolve in the 21st century, it will be essential to consider the interconnected nature of the global economy and the diverse perspectives and interests of countries, communities, and stakeholders around the world. By embracing sustainability, inclusivity, and innovation, capitalism can continue to adapt and thrive in a rapidly changing global landscape.

Chapter 7: Capitalism and Society

Capitalism and society have a deeply intertwined relationship, as capitalism shapes the economic, social, and cultural dynamics of societies around the world. Capitalism, as an economic system based on private ownership of the means of production and the pursuit of profit, has both positive and negative impacts on society.

One of the key ways capitalism impacts society is through economic growth and development. Capitalism has been credited with driving economic growth, creating jobs, and increasing living standards for millions of people around the world. By incentivizing innovation, entrepreneurship, and investment, capitalism has enabled societies to harness human creativity and ingenuity to create wealth and prosperity. Moreover, capitalism has facilitated the efficient allocation of resources, specialization of labor, and expansion of markets, leading to increased productivity and economic efficiency.

Education and Opportunity

When examining the relationship between capitalism and society, education and opportunity emerge as critical components. Education acts as a catalyst for social mobility, economic prosperity, and individual empowerment within capitalist societies, playing a pivotal role in shaping opportunities for individuals to succeed and contribute to the economy.

In capitalist societies, education serves as a pathway to economic opportunity by equipping individuals with the knowledge, skills, and competencies needed to participate in the workforce and adapt to changing economic demands. Through education, individuals acquire foundational literacy and numeracy skills, as well as specialized knowledge and technical expertise in various fields such as science, technology, engineering, and mathematics (STEM), humanities, arts, and social sciences. This educational foundation enables individuals to pursue diverse career paths, from entry-level positions to advanced professional roles, and contribute to economic growth and innovation.

Moreover, education serves as a means of social mobility within capitalist societies, allowing individuals from diverse backgrounds to overcome socioeconomic barriers and achieve upward mobility. By providing access to quality education and training opportunities, capitalist societies can empower individuals to break the cycle of poverty, improve their economic circumstances, and achieve social advancement. Education enables individuals to pursue higher-paying jobs, access higher levels of education, and enter professions traditionally dominated by privileged groups, thus promoting greater equality of opportunity and social inclusion.

Additionally, education plays a crucial role in fostering entrepreneurship and innovation within capitalist societies. By providing individuals with the knowledge, skills, and resources needed to start and grow businesses, education cultivates a culture of entrepreneurship and innovation that drives economic dynamism and competitiveness. Entrepreneurial education equips individuals with the entrepreneurial mindset, problem-solving abilities, and business acumen needed to identify opportunities, develop innovative solutions, and create value in the marketplace. Moreover, education fosters a supportive ecosystem for entrepreneurship by providing access to mentorship, networking, and funding opportunities, thus enabling aspiring entrepreneurs to turn their ideas into successful ventures.

Furthermore, education contributes to human capital development and economic productivity within capitalist societies by enhancing workforce skills, productivity, and adaptability. As economies become increasingly knowledge-based and technology-driven, the demand for skilled workers with advanced education and training is on the rise. Education equips individuals with the critical thinking, communication, and collaboration skills needed to succeed in today's globalized and digitalized economy.

However, despite the potential of education to promote opportunity and social mobility, access to quality education remains unevenly distributed within capitalist societies, leading to disparities in educational attainment and outcomes. Socioeconomic factors such as income, race, ethnicity, gender, and geography often influence access to educational opportunities, leading to inequities in educational access, resources, and outcomes. Moreover, structural barriers such as inadequate funding, inadequate infrastructure, and systemic discrimination can further exacerbate educational inequalities, perpetuating cycles of disadvantage and inequality within society.

Education and opportunity are deeply interconnected within capitalist societies, with education serving as a catalyst for economic opportunity, social mobility, and individual empowerment. By providing access to quality education and training opportunities, capitalist societies can empower individuals to succeed in the workforce, achieve upward mobility, and contribute to economic growth and innovation. However, addressing educational inequalities and ensuring equitable access to educational opportunities are essential for realizing the full potential of education to promote opportunity and social inclusion within capitalist societies.

Healthcare and Welfare

In the relationship between capitalism and society, healthcare and welfare are significant components that deeply influence the well-being and stability of communities. Capitalist societies typically structure healthcare and welfare systems based on principles of market competition, individual responsibility, and private provision of services. While capitalism has brought advancements in healthcare and social welfare, it also poses challenges related to accessibility, affordability, and equity.

Healthcare is a fundamental aspect of societal well-being, and capitalist economies have seen significant advancements in medical technology, research, and treatment. In capitalist societies, healthcare systems often operate within a mixed-market framework, combining public and private sector involvement. Private healthcare providers offer services to those who can afford them, while government-funded programs, such as Medicare and Medicaid in the United States, provide coverage to vulnerable populations.

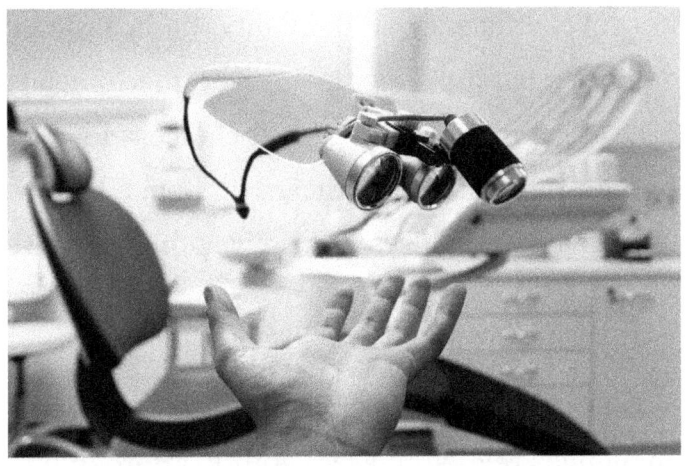

One of the key advantages of capitalist healthcare systems is innovation. Capitalism fosters competition among healthcare providers, pharmaceutical companies, and medical device manufacturers, driving innovation and technological advancements in medical treatments, drugs, and devices. This has led to breakthroughs in areas such as biotechnology, genomics, and personalized medicine, improving patient outcomes and quality of life.

Moreover, capitalism has the potential to improve efficiency and quality in healthcare delivery. By introducing market mechanisms such as competition, consumer choice, and price signals, capitalist healthcare systems aim to incentivize providers to deliver high-quality care at lower costs.

However, capitalist healthcare systems also face challenges related to accessibility, affordability, and equity. In a purely market-driven system, access to healthcare services may be limited to those who can afford them, leaving marginalized and low-income populations without adequate coverage. Healthcare costs, including insurance premiums, deductibles, and out-of-pocket expenses, can pose financial barriers to accessing care, leading to disparities in health outcomes based on socioeconomic status.

Furthermore, capitalist healthcare systems may prioritize profitability over public health outcomes, leading to inefficiencies, cost-cutting measures, and inadequate coverage for essential services. For-profit healthcare providers may prioritize treatments that yield higher profits over preventive care or treatments for chronic conditions.

In response to these challenges, many capitalist societies implement social welfare programs to provide a safety net for vulnerable populations. Welfare programs, such as social security, unemployment insurance, and food assistance, aim to mitigate poverty, reduce inequality, and promote social cohesion. These programs are funded through taxation and provide financial assistance to individuals and families facing economic hardship.

Moreover, capitalist societies often provide healthcare coverage through government-funded programs or private insurance systems. Universal healthcare systems, such as those found in countries like Canada, the United Kingdom, and Australia, provide comprehensive coverage to all residents, regardless of income or employment status. In contrast, other capitalist countries, such as the United States, rely on a mixed system of private and public insurance, where individuals may purchase coverage through private insurers or receive government-funded coverage through programs like Medicare and Medicaid.

Despite these efforts, welfare systems in capitalist societies face criticism for their complexity, bureaucracy, and inefficiency. Means-tested welfare programs may discourage individuals from working or saving by reducing benefits as income increases. Additionally, welfare fraud and abuse can undermine the effectiveness and sustainability of welfare programs, leading to calls for reform and stricter eligibility requirements.

In conclusion, healthcare and welfare are critical components of capitalist societies, influencing the well-being and stability of communities. While capitalism has brought advancements in medical technology and healthcare delivery, it also poses challenges related to accessibility, affordability, and equity. Social welfare programs aim to mitigate these challenges by providing a safety net for vulnerable populations, but they also face criticism for their complexity and inefficiency. Addressing these challenges requires a balance between market-driven innovation and social solidarity to ensure that all members of society have access to essential healthcare and welfare services.

Culture and Media

In the context of capitalism and society, culture and media play crucial roles in shaping values, perceptions, and behaviors, influencing the fabric of society and the functioning of capitalist economies. Capitalism interacts with culture and media in complex ways, with cultural industries operating within capitalist market economies while also reflecting and shaping societal norms, values, and identities.

Capitalism has a profound impact on culture, influencing the production, distribution, and consumption of cultural goods and services. In capitalist societies, cultural industries such as film, music, television, publishing, and advertising operate within market-driven systems, where profitability, competition, and consumer demand drive decision-making. As a result, cultural production often reflects commercial imperatives, with an emphasis on profitability, marketability, and mass appeal.

Moreover, capitalism promotes cultural diversity and creativity by fostering competition, innovation, and entrepreneurship within cultural industries. The capitalist marketplace provides opportunities for artists, creators, and cultural producers to express themselves, explore new ideas, and reach diverse audiences. Capitalist economies incentivize creativity and innovation through intellectual property rights, copyright protections, and market rewards, encouraging the production of original and commercially viable cultural products.

Furthermore, capitalism influences the distribution and consumption of cultural products through market mechanisms such as advertising, marketing, and distribution channels. In capitalist societies, media conglomerates, advertising agencies, and digital platforms play a significant role in shaping consumer preferences, influencing purchasing decisions, and controlling access to cultural content. Capitalist media industries prioritize profitability and audience engagement, leading to the proliferation of commercial content, branded entertainment, and consumer-driven media experiences.

However, capitalism also raises concerns about the commodification and commercialization of culture, as cultural products and experiences are increasingly treated as market commodities to be bought, sold, and consumed. The commercialization of culture can lead to the homogenization of cultural expression, as mainstream media and entertainment industries prioritize mass appeal and profit margins over artistic integrity, diversity, and authenticity. Moreover, capitalist media industries may perpetuate harmful stereotypes, promote consumerism, and reinforce unequal power dynamics within society.

Additionally, capitalism shapes the role of media in shaping public discourse, political participation, and social change. In capitalist societies, media outlets, both traditional and digital, play a crucial role in informing citizens, shaping public opinion, and holding governments and institutions accountable. However, capitalist media industries may also be influenced by corporate interests, political biases, and market pressures, leading to issues such as media consolidation, sensationalism, and misinformation.

Furthermore, capitalism influences the globalization of culture and media, as digital technologies and global markets facilitate the exchange of cultural products, ideas, and values across borders. Globalization has led to the spread of Western cultural norms and values, as well as the emergence of transnational media conglomerates and digital platforms with global reach. While globalization promotes cultural exchange and diversity, it also raises concerns about cultural imperialism, cultural hegemony, and the erosion of local cultures and identities.

Culture and media are deeply intertwined with capitalism, shaping and reflecting societal values, norms, and identities within capitalist societies. While capitalism promotes creativity, innovation, and cultural diversity within cultural industries, it also raises concerns about the commercialization, commodification, and homogenization of culture. Moreover, capitalism influences the role of media in shaping public discourse, political participation, and social change, with implications for democracy, citizenship, and cultural identity in the 21st century. Addressing these challenges requires a nuanced understanding of the complex interplay between capitalism, culture, and media, as well as efforts to promote diversity, inclusion, and ethical practices within cultural industries and media ecosystems.

Conclusion

"Freedom in Capitalism" delves into the complex relationship between freedom and capitalism, exploring how economic systems influence individual liberties and societal dynamics. Through a nuanced examination of historical examples and economic theory, the book elucidates the multifaceted nature of freedom within capitalist frameworks.

Throughout the text, the author articulates the idea that capitalism and freedom are inherently intertwined, with each system exerting profound influences on the other. Capitalism, characterized by private ownership of the means of production, market competition, and profit-seeking behavior, offers individuals opportunities for self-determination, entrepreneurship, and economic autonomy. By allowing individuals to pursue their own economic interests and ambitions, capitalism fosters a sense of agency and empowerment, empowering individuals to make choices about their lives and livelihoods.

Moreover, the book highlights how capitalism, by fostering innovation, economic growth, and prosperity, can expand the scope of individual freedoms and opportunities within society. Through the mechanisms of market competition and creative destruction, capitalism creates new possibilities for social mobility, wealth accumulation, and upward advancement, enabling individuals to transcend socioeconomic constraints and pursue their aspirations.

However, the book also acknowledges the complexities and contradictions inherent in capitalist systems, which can sometimes undermine individual freedoms and exacerbate social inequalities. Capitalism's emphasis on profit maximization and market efficiency can lead to exploitation, alienation, and unequal distribution of wealth and power, limiting the freedoms of marginalized and disadvantaged groups within society. Moreover, the concentration of economic power in the hands of a few wealthy individuals and corporations can erode democratic governance and political freedoms, leading to concerns about cronyism, corruption, and regulatory capture.

Furthermore, the book explores the role of government in safeguarding and promoting freedom within capitalist societies. While capitalism thrives on principles of limited government intervention and free-market competition, the book argues that certain regulatory mechanisms and social safety nets are necessary to ensure the protection of individual rights and liberties. Government intervention in areas such as antitrust regulation, consumer protection, and social welfare can mitigate the negative externalities of capitalism, promote fairness and equality, and safeguard basic human rights.

Lastly, "Freedom in Capitalism" offers a comprehensive analysis of the complex interplay between freedom and capitalism, highlighting both the opportunities and challenges inherent in capitalist systems. By examining the historical, economic, and philosophical dimensions of freedom within capitalist frameworks, the book deepens our understanding of how economic systems shape individual liberties and societal dynamics. Ultimately, the book underscores the importance of fostering a balance between economic freedom and social responsibility, ensuring that capitalism serves as a force for human flourishing and democratic governance.

www.ingramcontent.com/pod-product-compliance
Lightning Source LLC
Chambersburg PA
CBHW050301230526
45471CB00005B/1967